THE ROAD LESS TRAVELED

The Road Less Traveled

Unique Destinations Around the World

B. VINCENT

QuantumQuill Press

CONTENTS

Introduction: Embracing the Journey to the Unseen and Unknown

In a world overflowing with a desire for new experiences, where the reverberations of strides can be heard in the most remote corners, there exists a way less trampled, winding through the concealed and the unexplored world. This book is a tribute to that way, an aide for the spirit longing to break liberated from the recognizable and dive into the profundities of the unknown. It's for the people who look for to consider the world to be well as to encounter it in its generally crude and unfiltered structure.

The Charm of the Less common direction

The less common direction isn't simply a way; an excursion challenges the soul and flashes the creative mind. In the period of web-based entertainment, where each unlikely treasure appears to have been uncovered, the mission for special objections turns into a more profound quest for importance and association. There the story shifts from the quantity of likes to the individual changes that happen when you wind up in a new land, where each sense is stirred, and each second holds the commitment of another revelation.

The Benefit of Investigating the New

Investigating the new is a practice in modesty and development. It instructs us that magnificence and miracle don't live exclusively in the spots celebrated by postcards and travel guides. All things being equal, they prosper in the calm corners of the world, in the accounts of individuals who have seen the walk of time and the dance of the components, yet stay immaculate by the furor of advancement. These objections offer an actual getaway as well as an entry to a reality where time moves in an unexpected way, welcoming us to dial back, reflect, and maybe rediscover portions of ourselves lost in the hustle of regular daily existence.

Finding Sorcery in the Edges

This book takes you on a journey to the edges of the guide, where the wizardry of disclosure actually resides. It's tied in with wandering into the core of Eastern Europe, where old palaces murmur stories from times gone past against a setting of moving slopes and spiritualist timberlands. It's tied in with looking for Aurora Borealis in Scandinavia, where the sky turns into a material for nature's most breathtaking light show. It's tied in with tracking down comfort on the less popular isles of the Mediterranean, where the ocean sings bedtime songs of old civilizations.

The Excursion Inside

In any case, maybe, the most significant disclosures on this excursion are not just about the spots we visit. They are about the appearance in the reflection of our spirits when we get out of our usual ranges of familiarity. They are about the fellowships manufactured in the fire of shared encounters, the consideration of outsiders who become the overseers of our recollections, and the acknowledgment that the world is undeniably more gorgeous and complex than we might have at any point envisioned.

A Challenge to Experience

This presentation is a greeting — a challenge to look into the great beyond, to look for excellence in the shadows and stories in the quietness. It's a consolation to step outside of what might be expected, as an explorer, however as a searcher of the horde bits of insight that untruth holding up on the planet's secret corners.

As you turn these pages, let each word be a stage on your own excursion to the concealed and obscure. Allow this book to be a compass directing you to the core of what it means to genuinely investigate — to set out on an excursion that will take you across the globe, yet in addition more profound into the pith of your courageous soul.

Get ready to leave on this excursion, to embrace the less common direction, and to find the special objections that anticipate all over the planet.

| 1 |

Europe: A Tapestry of Hidden Gems

Europe, with its rich history and different scenes, offers a mosaic of social and regular miracles. Past its popular capitals lies a gold mine of less popular objections, each with a special story to tell. This part investigates the unexpected, yet invaluable treasures of Eastern Europe, the regular peculiarities of Scandinavia, and the serene isles of the Mediterranean, displaying the magnificence that anticipates the inquisitive explorer able to wander outside of what might be expected.

2.1 Eastern Europe's Unlikely treasures

Eastern Europe is a domain where history and culture interweave in the midst of scenes that rouse both stunningness and reflection. Here, old palaces stand as sentinels over lands that have seen the section of realms, while the glow of its kin welcomes you into an existence where custom and advancement dance together as one.

•Lviv, Ukraine: Frequently eclipsed by its bigger partners, Lviv is a city where craftsmanship, culture, and history combine in an energetic mosaic. Its UNESCO-recorded Old Town is a demonstration of structural splendor, with impacts going from Renaissance to Craftsmanship Nouveau. Bistros and bookshops line its cobblestone roads, welcoming guests to encounter the spirit of Ukrainian cordiality.

•Sibiu, Romania: Settled in the core of Transylvania, Sibiu is a city where old stories and innovation mix consistently. Its middle age walls and pinnacles watch extremely old legends, while its energetic squares and celebrations commend the persevering through soul of the Romanian public. The close by Carpathian Mountains offer a break into nature, with trails prompting stunning vistas and detached towns.

•Rila Cloister, Bulgaria: Stowed away in the tranquil Rila Mountains, the Rila Religious community is a profound safe-haven known for its dazzling frescoes and Byzantine design. This UNESCO World Legacy site isn't simply a position of strict importance; it's a window into Bulgaria's spirit, offering serenity and motivation to all who visit.

2.2 Aurora Borealis and Then some: Scandinavia

Scandinavia is a place that is known for contrasts, where the 12 PM sun meets the haziness of winter, making normal exhibitions that draw explorers from around the world. Past the charm of Aurora Borealis, this district flaunts scenes that reach from verdant woods to rough shores, each offering exceptional encounters for the gutsy soul.

•Lofoten Islands, Norway: The Lofoten Islands are an emotional mix of mountain tops, profound fjords, and fishing towns that appear to oppose the components. Here, Aurora Borealis dance across the sky in winter, while summer brings vast days and amazing open doors for climbing, fishing, and investigating the pristine nature.

•Abisko, Sweden: Known as perhaps of the best spot on the planet to observe Aurora Borealis, Abisko is likewise a shelter for open air fans. Its public park offers trails that navigate through flawless Nordic scenes, with opportunities to recognize natural life and experience the Sami culture.

•Koli Public Park, Finland: Koli Public Park is a scene of moving slopes and clear lakes that roused numerous Finnish craftsmen and writers. It's where quiet is a language, welcoming guests to associate with nature through climbing, skiing, or basically taking in the all encompassing perspectives from on Ukko-Koli Slope.

2.3 The Mediterranean's Less popular Isles

The Mediterranean Ocean is dabbed with islands that are universes regardless of anyone else's opinion, each offering a novel mix of history, culture, and regular magnificence. Past the very much trampled objections, there are isles where life moves at the beat of the ocean, offering a brief look into the Mediterranean soul.

•Vis, Croatia: A long way from the hordes of Dubrovnik and Divided lies the island of Vis, a diamond that has held its pristine appeal. Known for its staggering sea shores, perfectly clear waters, and delicious fish, Vis is a safe house for those looking for comfort and credibility.

•Pantelleria, Italy: Nearer to Africa than the Italian central area, Pantelleria is an island of rough magnificence, known for its volcanic scenes, warm springs, and escapade fields. It's where effortlessness is the quintessence of extravagance, welcoming guests to submerge themselves in the serenity of Mediterranean life.

•Sifnos, Greece: With its whitewashed towns, cerulean oceans, and culinary enjoyments, Sifnos epitomizes the quintessential Greek island enchant. Away from the hustle of vacationer areas of interest, it offers a quiet retreat with unblemished sea shores, climbing trails, and a rich social legacy.

| 2 |

Asia: Where Ancient Meets Modern

Asia, a landmass of unrivaled variety, offers a mix of history, culture, and normal magnificence that entices the spirit of each and every voyager. From the peaceful sea shores and rough piles of Southeast Asia to the old urban communities and immense scenes of Focal Asia, and the unseen social fortunes of the Center East, Asia presents an embroidery of encounters that blow some minds.

3.1 Southeast Asia's Mystery Sea shores and Mountains

Southeast Asia is eminent for its dynamic societies, rich scenes, and verifiable destinations. Past the notable locations lies a universe of unlikely treasures where quietness and excellence rule.

•El Nido, Palawan, Philippines: Frequently refered to for its perfectly clear waters and glorious limestone precipices, El Nido offers more going on than might be immediately obvious. Secret tidal ponds, secret sea shores, and immaculate coral reefs give a safe-haven to those looking for isolation and experience.

•Luang Prabang, Laos: This UNESCO World Legacy city is a mix of customary Lao wooden houses and European frontier engineering, set at the juncture of the Mekong and Nam Khan streams. Past its tranquil excellence, Luang Prabang is a door to local cascades, caverns, and ethnic towns.

•Hsipaw, Myanmar: A long way from the vacationer trails, Hsipaw offers a legitimate look into country Burmese life. Traveling across the encompassing slopes uncovers cascades, natural aquifers, and old pagodas, with the potential chance to remain in nearby towns.

3.2 Focal Asia's Antiquated Urban areas and Scenes

Focal Asia, with its immense steppes and old urban communities, is a district where history is scratched into the scene. Here, voyagers can step back in time and investigate the leftovers of the Silk Street that once associated the East and West.

•Samarkand, Uzbekistan: Samarkand is a city where history wakes up, with its staggering Islamic engineering and old shipping lanes. The Registan Square, with its three madrasahs, is a feature, displaying the city's verifiable importance and design excellence.

•Almaty, Kazakhstan: Settled in the lower regions of the Trans-Ili Alatau mountains, Almaty is a city where innovation and nature exist together. The close by Charyn Gulch offers a characteristic departure, with shocking vistas and remarkable stone developments.

•Pamir Thruway, Tajikistan: One of the world's most grand drives, the Pamir Roadway navigates the rough scenes of the Pamir Mountains. It offers a remarkable excursion through far off towns, high-height lakes, and a portion of the planet's most fantastic vistas.

3.3 The Center East's Unseen Social Fortunes

The Center East is a support of civilizations, where old history and present day life interlace. Past the titles, the locale flaunts social fortunes and normal ponders that remain generally unseen by the more extensive world.

•Musandam Landmass, Oman: Frequently alluded to as the "Norway of Arabia," the Musandam Promontory is famous for its fjord-like khors, completely clear waters, and emotional mountain landscape. Dhow travels offer an exceptional viewpoint on this staggering scene.

•Mardin, Turkey: Roosted on a slope sitting above the Mesopotamian fields, Mardin is a city where stone-cut structures and winding roads recount the narrative of its different social legacy. It's where history is alive in the design, food, and customs.

•Socotra Island, Yemen: Known as the "Galapagos of the Indian Sea," Socotra Island is home to one of a kind greenery, including the notorious Mythical beast's Blood Tree. Its seclusion has safeguarded a one of a kind biological system and a lifestyle that is a window into nature's variety.

| 3 |

Africa: Beyond the Beaten Path

Africa, a landmass of stunning variety and stunning magnificence, offers more than the very much trampled safaris and the superb scenes frequently featured in movement handouts. This section digs into the core of Africa's less popular objections, investigating the off in an unexpected direction undertakings that anticipate those able to wander past the natural. From detached safari encounters to island heavens and the hypnotizing deserts and societies of the north, Africa's unexpected, yet invaluable treasures are a demonstration of the landmass' rich and differed embroidery of encounters.

4.1 Safari Outside of what might be expected: Past the Large Five

While Africa is inseparable from safari undertakings, there's a world past the famous stores where the wild welcomes you into a cozy hit the dance floor with nature, away from the groups.

•Mana Pools Public Park, Zimbabwe: Assigned an UNESCO World Legacy site, Mana Pools is prestigious for its normal excellence and extensive variety of natural life. Its exceptional scene, portrayed by riverine timberlands, tremendous floodplains, and the background of the Zambezi Waterway, offers one of the landmass' most wonderful safari encounters, with open doors for strolling safaris and kayaking.

•Liuwa Plain Public Park, Zambia: Most popular for its marvelous wildebeest movement, Liuwa Plain is an unlikely treasure that offers a select experience with nature. The recreation area's tremendous, open savannas are home to a rich embroidery of birds and creatures, remembering the second-biggest wildebeest movement for Africa, giving a safari experience that feels both individual and significant.

•Gonarezhou Public Park, Zimbabwe: Signifying "Spot of Elephants," Gonarezhou is essential for the Incomparable Limpopo Transfrontier Park. It's a place that is known for immaculate magnificence, with transcending baobabs, sandstone precipices, and a wealth of natural life. The recreation area's tough landscape offers a safari experience for those looking for isolation and experience.

4.2 Island Heavens of the Indian Sea

The Indian Sea is dotted with islands that offer a break into paradisiacal scenes where the beat of the ocean establishes the rhythm of life.

•Intrusive Be, Madagascar: Off the northwest bank of Madagascar, Meddling Be is an island of volcanic lakes, lavish ylang manors, and rich coral reefs. Known as the "Fragrance Island," its warm waters and various environments make it an ideal objective for those hoping to jump, fish, or basically absorb the peaceful island climate.

•Lamu, Kenya: Lamu, an UNESCO World Legacy site, is Kenya's most seasoned living town, offering a brief look into extremely old Swahili culture. With its sans vehicle roads, conventional dhows cruising in the harbor, and lovely sea shores, Lamu gives a tranquil retreat into a more slow speed of life.

•Mnemba Island, Tanzania: Mnemba Island is a restrictive island escape encompassed by the reasonable blue waters of the Indian Sea. Its coral atoll is famous for fantastic swimming and jumping potential open doors, with flourishing coral reefs and a rich marine life that incorporates whale sharks and dolphins.

4.3 The Deserts and Societies of Northern Africa

Northern Africa's scenes are basically as different as its societies, offering a mix of verifiable extravagance and regular miracle that charms the heart and brain.

•Siwa Desert spring, Egypt: Settled in the Western Desert, Siwa Desert spring is a safe-haven of old olive forests, palm trees, and completely clear springs. This far off desert spring isn't just a characteristic retreat yet in addition a social one, home to the Siwi public and a rich history that incorporates the Prophet of Amun, visited by Alexander the Incomparable.

•The Sahara Desert, Morocco: Past the clamoring souks and energetic urban areas lies the serenity of the Sahara Desert. A camel journey into the hills of Erg Chebbi or Erg Chigaga offers an extraordinary experience under the stars, where the quietness of the desert says a lot.

•Djenné, Mali: Home to the Incomparable Mosque of Djenné, the world's biggest mud-block building, Djenné is a verifiable city that has kept up with its social legacy and engineering. Its Monday market, a social event that draws individuals from everywhere the district, is an energetic showcase of Mali's social variety.

| 4 |

The Americas: A Journey Through the Uncharted

The Americas, extending from the frigid scenes of the Cold toward the southern tips of Patagonia, offer a mind boggling variety of encounters for explorers looking for ways more uncommon. This part investigates the secret archeological locales of South America, the wild, immaculate scenes of North America, and the mystery getaways of Focal America and the Caribbean, every location offering its own exceptional mix of experience, culture, and normal excellence.

5.1 South America's Secret Archeological Locales

South America, a mainland wealthy in history and culture, is home to a portion of the world's most huge archeological fortunes, a significant number of which lie past the recognizable paths.

•Choquequirao, Peru: Frequently alluded to as the 'sister city' of Machu Picchu, Choquequirao is a less popular Incan city that offers an extraordinary look into the past, without the groups. Open simply by a difficult trip, its far off area and stunning perspectives across the Apurimac Valley cause it a remunerating venture for the individuals who to embrace it.

•Tiwanaku, Bolivia: Arranged close to Lake Titicaca, Tiwanaku is an old city that originates before the Incan Realm. Its vestiges, including the renowned Passage of the Sun, offer a window into a development that thrived well before the appearance of Europeans in the Americas. The site's solid designs and perplexing carvings stay a subject of interest and secret.

•San Agustín, Colombia: Settled in the Andean lower regions, San Agustín is home to north of 500 solid sculptures and models that date back to the first to the eighth hundreds of years. This UNESCO World Legacy site offers a remarkable knowledge into the strict and social designs of a pre-Columbian culture, with its cryptic stone figures monitoring the mysteries of a lost human progress.

5.2 North America's Wild, Immaculate Scenes

North America's immense scenes are a demonstration of the landmass' normal marvels, offering immaculate wild regions that entice the courageous soul.

•Torngat Mountains Public Park, Canada: In the northern compasses of Labrador lies Torngat Mountains Public Park, a tough scene where polar bears meander, and Aurora Borealis dance across the sky. The recreation area's distant excellence and otherworldly importance to the Inuit public make it a position of significant normal miracle.

•Limit Waters Kayak Region Wild, USA: Extending along the line among Minnesota and Canada, the Limit Waters Kayak Region Wild proposals more than 1,000,000 sections of land of perfect streams and woodlands. Its segregated lakes and streams give an unrivaled chance to paddling, fishing, and associating with nature peacefully and isolation.

•Valley of Destruction, Dominica: Totally unrelated to its Caribbean namesake, Dominica's Valley of Devastation is a volcanic scene of bubbling mud pools, fumaroles, and natural aquifers. Climbing through this supernatural territory offers an exceptional experience, coming full circle in the mitigating waters of the Bubbling Lake, one of the world's biggest underground aquifers.

5.3 Focal America and Caribbean's Mystery Getaways

The tropical scenes of Focal America and the Caribbean conceal various disconnected places where voyagers can encounter the locale's regular excellence and energetic societies from the vacationer swarms.

•Little Corn Island, Nicaragua: Distant from the hustle of central area life, Little Corn Island is a heaven of white sandy sea shores, completely clear waters, and lavish tropical woodlands. Without any vehicles permitted on the island, it's a safe house for those looking for harmony and a genuine Caribbean vibe.

•Semuc Champey, Guatemala: Concealed somewhere down in the Guatemalan wilderness, Semuc Champey is a characteristic limestone span that traverses a waterway, making a progression of shocking turquoise pools. The far off area and the excursion through the rich scene make it a supernatural break for nature sweethearts.

•Saba, Netherlands Antilles: Frequently neglected for its more popular neighbors, Saba is a volcanic island that ascents steeply from the sea. Known as "The Untainted Sovereign" of the Caribbean, its rough territory is home to remarkable climbing trails, various biological systems, and the absolute best-saved coral reefs in the locale.

| 5 |

Oceania: Discovering the Uncharted

Oceania, a tremendous territory of the Pacific Sea spotted with islands, offers probably the most different and staggering scenes in the world. From the rough outback of Australia to the quiet excellence of New Zealand's mountains and fjords, and the immaculate, distant islands of the Pacific, this segment investigates the more unfamiliar streets that lead to stunning revelations.

6.1 Australia's Outback and Failed to remember Shores

Australia, a place that is known for unmistakable differences and normal marvels, welcomes swashbucklers to investigate its heartland and shorelines, where the pith of the mainland's magnificence and soul of the wild are tangible.

•The Kimberley, Western Australia: The Kimberley is one of Australia's last wild boondocks, known for its glorious cascades, profound canyons, and the old Fumble Mishandle Reach. Going through this remote scene, whether by all wheel drive, by walking, or by means of a beautiful flight, offers an extraordinary look into the country's tough magnificence and Native legacy.

•Cape York Promontory, Queensland: For those able to handle the difficult excursion, Cape York Landmass offers an experience to quite possibly of Australia's most immaculate locale. From the red soil of the outback to the rich rainforests and flawless sea shores, it's where you can genuinely detach and drench yourself in the normal world.

•Kangaroo Island, South Australia: Frequently neglected for additional popular locations, Kangaroo Island is a safe-haven for untamed life and normal magnificence. With its exceptional stone developments, similar to the Momentous Rocks and Naval commanders Curve, local untamed life including kangaroos, koalas, and seals, and a flourishing neighborhood food and wine scene, it's a microcosm of Australia's different attractions.

6.2 New Zealand's Less popular Normal Marvels

New Zealand, known as Aotearoa, the place that is known for the long white cloud, is a nation where nature's magnificence is on full presentation, from the North Island toward the South Island, offering an excursion into scenes that motivate stunningness and peacefulness.

•The Catlins, South Island: The Catlins locale offers a rough and remote experience, with its wild shorelines, thick backwoods, and secret cascades. Features incorporate Chunk Point with its notable beacon and the froze backwoods of Doodad Narrows. It's where natural life experiences, including penguins and ocean lions, add to the wizardry of the investigation.

•Tongariro Northern Circuit, North Island: While the Tongariro Snow capped Crossing is notable, the full Northern Circuit offers a more profound jump into the volcanic heart of the North Island. This multi-day climb takes globe-trotters past emerald lakes, dynamic volcanoes, and through remarkable snow capped glades, offering a difficult however remunerating experience.

•Stewart Island/Rakiura: Frequently missed by guests to New Zealand, Stewart Island offers an unmatched chance to encounter New Zealand's wild. With its bountiful birdlife, including the kiwi, which can be seen right at home, and the Rakiura Track, one of New Zealand's Extraordinary Strolls, it's a shelter for nature sweethearts and those looking for isolation.

6.3 The Pacific Islands' Strange Domains

The Pacific Islands, dissipated like gems across the immense sea, are home to societies saturated with custom and islands of immaculate magnificence, offering tranquil escapes and undertakings in equivalent measure.

•The Solomon Islands: With its rich WWII history, lively coral reefs, and thick wildernesses, the Solomon Islands remain generally off the standard traveler radar. The islands offer staggering open doors for plunging, surfing, and social inundation, giving a brief look into a lifestyle that has stayed unaltered for quite a long time.

•Vanuatu's Tanna Island: Tanna Island is popular for Mount Yasur, one of the world's most open dynamic volcanoes. Past the fountain of liquid magma, Tanna's customary towns, wonderful sea shores, and the puzzling Blue Cavern offer a more profound comprehension of Vanuatu's regular excellence and social wealth.

•The Cook Islands: While Rarotonga is the most visited of the Cook Islands, the external islands offer immaculate heaven. Aitutaki's tidal pond, one of the most gorgeous on the planet, and the untainted magnificence and old Polynesian culture of Atiu, are only a sample of the quietness and experience that anticipates in this Pacific heaven.

Conclusion: Reflecting on the Uncharted Path

As our excursion through the pages of this book comes to a nearby, we end up remaining at the edge of incalculable streets more uncommon, each enticing with the commitment of unseen marvels and individual disclosures. From the unlikely treasures of Eastern Europe to the quiet islands of the Pacific, the unfamiliar way has offered us a brief look into the core of our planet's different scenes and societies. It has shown us that past the recognizable skylines of very much trampled objections lies a world overflowing with experience, ready to be investigated by those trying courageous to wander off in an unexpected direction.

The Substance of Investigation

Investigation isn't just about the objections we visit; about the excursion inside ourselves unfurls as we cross these obscure ways. It's about the strength we find when confronted with difficulties, the lowliness we learn within the sight of societies and chronicles immensely unique in relation to our own, and the feeling of miracle that reignites inside us as we experience the regular and man-made wonders of our reality.

A Call to Experience

This book is a call to experience — a reference point for those longing to break liberated from the imperatives of routine and leave on an excursion of revelation. It's a challenge to move back from the advanced interruptions and the commotion of regular daily existence, to track down comfort in the isolation of the desert, the magnificence of old vestiges, or the quietness of an immaculate ocean side. It's an update that the world is huge, its secrets various, and its excellence limitless, anticipating those with the mental fortitude to search them out.

Making Recollections and Building Scaffolds

The ways more uncommon are not simply courses on a guide; they are the tales that we'll convey with us long after our strides have blurred. They are the recollections that will make us feel good inside and the examples that will shape our viewpoints. By picking the less common direction, we find our general surroundings as well as manufacture further associations with individuals we meet en route, building extensions of understanding and fellowship across the partitions of language, culture, and geology.

The Ceaseless Excursion

As you close this book, may you see it not as an end but rather as the start of your own strange excursion. May the objections and encounters chronicled inside these pages motivate you to gather your sacks, ribbon up your boots, and set out on an undertaking that will lead you to the concealed and the unexplored world. Keep in mind, the most significant excursions are those that change us, leaving us perpetually different by the excellence and variety of the world we share.

Embrace the Excursion Ahead

In this way, to the brave spirits who really hope for far off shores and to the people who look for the enchanted that lies just into the great beyond — embrace the excursion ahead. Allow interest to be your compass and fortitude your aide as you set out on the less common direction. For it is on this way that the genuine substance of investigation is found, and the best experiences are conceived.

Appendices

The supplements act as a useful aide and asset for those prepared to leave on their excursion to the more uncommon objections all over the planet. Here, you'll track down tips for off in an unexpected direction travel and assets for additional investigation, guaranteeing you're exceptional for the experiences ahead.

8.1 Practical Tips for Off-the-Beaten-Path Travel

- Research Thoroughly: Before you go, research your destination for insights on local customs, weather, and any travel advisories. Look for blogs or forums where travelers share firsthand experiences.
- Travel Light: Pack only what you need, focusing on versatile clothing and essential gear. A lighter pack means easier mobility across diverse terrains.
- Learn Basic Phrases: Knowing basic phrases in the local language can greatly enhance your travel experience, making it easier to connect with locals and navigate unfamiliar areas.
- Embrace Flexibility: Traveling off the beaten path often requires flexibility. Be open to changing plans due to weather, local events, or opportunities for unique experiences.
- Stay Safe: Always let someone know your itinerary and check-in regularly. Invest in a good travel insurance policy that covers activities you plan to undertake.
- Support Local: Where possible, choose local accommodations, eat at local restaurants, and hire local guides. It enriches your travel experience and contributes to the local economy.

- Leave No Trace: Respect the natural environment and local cultures. Minimize your impact by following Leave No Trace principles and local guidelines.

8.2 Resources for Further Exploration

- Books and Guides: Look for travel books and guides dedicated to off-the-beaten-path destinations. Lonely Planet's "Off the Beaten Path" series offers insights into lesser-known areas.
- Online Forums and Blogs: Platforms like TripAdvisor, Lonely Planet forums, and travel blogs can provide valuable, up-to-date information from fellow travelers.
- Cultural Exchange Programs: Programs like Workaway and WWOOF offer opportunities to work and live with locals, offering a unique perspective on local life.
- Language Learning Tools: Apps like Duolingo and Babbel can help you learn basic phrases and more, enhancing communication with locals.
- Safety and Health Information: Websites like the CDC (Centers for Disease Control and Prevention) and WHO (World Health Organization) provide health advisories and vaccination recommendations for travelers.
- Local Tourism Boards: Many destinations have official tourism websites with resources for visitors, including information on attractions, accommodations, and local customs.
- Navigation Tools: Apps like Google Maps and Maps.me offer downloadable maps for offline use, which can be invaluable in areas with limited internet access.